WADING AND SHORE BIRDS
Roger S. Everett

1469 Morstein Road
West Chester, Pennsylvania 19380

Short—billed dowitcher

This book is dedicated to

Jeni, Jessi, Jonathan and Adrienne
They can now see the results of Papa's many trips to the marshes and
the beaches with his camera.

Printed in the United States of America.
ISBN: 0-88740-132-5
Published by Schiffer Publishing Ltd.
1469 Morstein Road, West Chester, Pennsylvania 19380

This book may be purchased from the publisher.
Please include $2.00 postage.
Try your bookstore first.

Acknowledgments

To Unto Savolainen, Bob Darling and the late Teuvo
Santala whose encouragement and critique showed me
that photography was exciting and challenging.

To Bessie Clifford whose yard full of birds created the
interest that led to my specializing in bird photography.

To Priscilla and Wallace Bailey, Dick Forster, Blair
Nikula and Bob Prescott for their patience in identifying
birds in my slides and for their assistance in teaching me
where to find birds on Cape Cod.

To Doug Congdon-Martin for his idea that this book
was a possibility.

And especially to Corinne for her love and support
which made this book a reality.

WADING BIRDS

GREAT BLUE HERON. A wonderful photographic subject as it silently fishes along the marsh creeks.

Every so often you'll see the Great Blue Heron fly to the edge of the marsh, perch on a tree limb and begin to preen.

As you can see by the snow and ice, the Great Blue Heron has become a year-round resident of many marshes, including this one on Cape Cod.

GREEN HERON. This small dark heron fishes in the marsh grass along the edges of ponds, and is usually seen with its neck tucked in ready to snap out and grab a fish.

The Green
Heron's neck
stretches way
out when it is
alarmed, making
it look almost
like a completely
different bird.

GLOSSY IBIS. This dark green bird is usually seen in later summer in northern marshes.

AMERICAN BITTERN. It is amazing how this large bird can remain so well hidden, sometimes only a few feet from where you are standing.

An unusual winter photograph of an American Bittern.

LEAST BITTERN. This very timid bird, found hiding in marsh grass, takes great patience and a little luck to photograph.

SORA. A small, chunky rail, with a yellow bill, seen running among the reeds.

This photo results from a lucky opportunity when the Sora stops
in an opening. Note the big feet.

VIRGINIA RAIL. A dark rail about the same size as the Sora, but even more secretive. I've been with people who can "call" rails out of hiding.

COMMON SNIPE. A long-billed wader that moves slowly among the reeds. This is a fall regular on Cape Cod.

You'll need patience to wait until the Snipe comes into the open.
Most views will be through the marsh grass.

WHIMBREL. A large sandpiper that is a summer regular in northern marshes.

LESSER YELLOW LEGS. This large sandpiper is common in northern marshes in the summer and early fall. It is easy to photograph if you remain still.

GREATER YELLOWLEGS. The Greater Yellowlegs looks like the Lesser but is larger and has a longer bill that is slightly upturned.

WILSON'S PHALAROPE-Male.

WILSON'S PHALAROPE-Female. A favorite with women birders, the female Wilson's Phalarope has all the beautiful plumage in the Spring while the male wears a dull light grey coloring.

BLACK CROWNED NIGHT HERON. This heron is a pond fisherman. Immatures in left photo, and an adult above.

This winter photo was taken at Orleans on Cape Cod. The Black Crowned Night Herons run into trouble finding food if there is a lengthy period of freezing temperatures.

SNOWY EGRET. A small white heron with a black bill, black legs and yellow "shoes." It is very entertaining as it shuffles its feet to stir up food, then jumps about with its wings flapping, catching each morsel.

The Snowy Egret often gathers in rather large flocks along the shore.

SHORE BIRDS

LEAST SANDPIPER. A small "peep" that is very common in the spring and summer, the Least Sandpiper is browner than the other small sandpipers and has greenish-yellow legs.

UPLAND SANDPIPER. Though this is a sandpiper, it is not found where other sandpipers are, preferring fields and open meadows.

SEMIPALMATED SANDPIPER. Often confused with the Least
Sandpiper, it is lighter in color and has black legs and bill.

Like most small "peeps" the semipalmated sandpiper runs along
the beach as if it were a wind-up toy.

SPOTTED SANDPIPER. A small sandpiper that teeters up and down as it runs along the edge of the water.

It is best to identify the Spotted Sandpiper by its characteristic walk because often you will see an "unspotted" Spotted Sandpiper.

STILT SANDPIPER (Immature). Not as common, this sandpiper
is heavily striped with a rust colored cheek.

I most often see the Stilt Sandpiper feeding among a group of
larger Yellowlegs.

SOLITARY SANDPIPER. An uncommon visitor at Cape Cod shores, this sandpiper is identified by its white eye-ring.

In this photo the Solitary Sandpiper also shows its beautiful
black and white tail feathers.

WHITE-RUMPED SANDPIPER. The wing-tips of this sandpiper extend beyond the rump more than on any other common type.

This photo shows some of the white-rump, but it is best seen when the bird is flying.

PECTORAL SANDPIPER. This beautifully marked bird is a bit larger than the other common sandpipers.

To fully appreciate the markings on the Pectoral Sandpiper you must see the striped bib from the front.

This photo shows the back of the Pectoral Sandpiper giving you each perspective.

SANDERLING. Not as common as the Least and Semipalmated Sandpipers, this bird is still quite numerous. It has more color in the summer with richer rust tones.

The Sanderling is more abundant in the fall around Cape Cod as
it returns as a white bird with black markings.

SHORT-BILLED DOWITCHER. Despite its name this is actually a long billed shore bird that feeds in the mud flats.

Note the rusty color and eye stripe on the Short-billed Dowitcher.

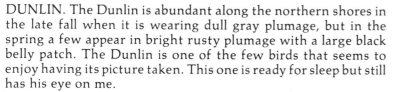

DUNLIN. The Dunlin is abundant along the northern shores in the late fall when it is wearing dull gray plumage, but in the spring a few appear in bright rusty plumage with a large black belly patch. The Dunlin is one of the few birds that seems to enjoy having its picture taken. This one is ready for sleep but still has his eye on me.

RED KNOT. Another abundant shorebird that wears bright colors in the summer and returns in the fall in a grey coat. It is stockier than the other shore birds.I think the markings on the Red Knot in the fall are more beautiful than any other shore bird. I've tried to capture it in this photograph.

BLACK-BELLIED PLOVER. Very abundant in large flocks especially on the Monomoy Islands off Cape Cod, it wears a very black breast in the summer which begins to fade as fall approaches.

By late fall the Black-bellied Plover's breast has become almost
white.

LESSER GOLDEN PLOVER. Look closely at the large flocks of Black-bellied Plovers and you may find one or two Goldens. We seldom see them in spring plumage but they come our way as wanderers in the fall. Their brown coloring stands out from their black and white relatives.

PIPING PLOVER. The Piping Plover is Cape Cod's endangered species, which all bird lovers are trying to protect. Its light sandy color works against it as a camouflage when dealing with humans. This timid little bird arrives in early spring, scrapes a nest and lays its eggs in the sand on the beaches which will become populated with humans in the summer.

When people come to Cape Cod on Memorial Day weekend with their dogs and off-road vehicles they cannot see this bird and its eggs. Volunteers set up fences and flags around the nesting areas, but this only works when people honor these signals.

SEMIPALMATED PLOVER. An abundant little shore bird, the
Semipalmated Plover is the one that tends to come closest to
check on you. The adult has black neck bands and an orange bill.
The younger ones are browner and have a dark bill.

RUDDY TURNSTONE. A chunky colorful shorebird, the Ruddy Turnstone lives up to its name. It turns over stones on the beach in search of food.

RUDDY TURNSTONE—Immature.

HUDSONIAN GODWIT. A large bird with a long upturned thin bill. Monomoy Island off Cape Cod has a flat muddy area that is called "Godwit Bar" because it is a regular summer stopping place for this shorebird.

Hudsonian Godwits stay together in small groups. Note the broad white band on its tail which is very visible in flight.

MARBLED GODWIT. Look closely at the Godwit groups and you may see one or two Marbled Godwits. It is a slightly larger bird and lighter in color with a longer and redder bill. On the next page you will see the Marbled with a group of Hudsonians. It is the third from the left.

WILLET. You will know when you are approaching a Willet nesting area as this good-sized bird noisily dive-bombs you, then it will land a few feet away and scold you for coming so close.

AMERICAN OYSTERCATCHER. It is an unusual looking bird and is easy to identify. Its piercing "wheep" announces its arrival.

The American Oystercatcher is even more spectacular in flight.

BLACK SKIMMER. The Black Skimmer's unusual red bill is
specially designed so they can fish on the fly.

Once in a while an immature Black Skimmer can be seen.

RUFF (left) and LONG-BILLED CURLEW (right). The two birds shown here, were photographed on Cape Cod where they are extremely rare.